# This Book Belongs To:

.....................................................................................................................

.....................................................................................................................

.....................................................................................................................

Date

You will teach me the right way to live.
Just being with you will bring complete happiness.
Being at your right side will make me happy forever.
• Psalm 16:11 ERV •

# Themes in This Book

- Family
- Salvation In Christ
- Prayer
- Rest In The Lord
- Children And Parents
- Faithfulness Of God
- Resting In God When Overwhelmed
- God's Word Is Perfect
- Encouragement
- Thankfulness
- God's Word Lives Forever
- Praising God

- Presence Of God
- Trusting In The Lord
- Worship
- God Is Perfect
- Loving God
- Following God
- God's Love For Us
- Joy
- Following Jesus
- Friendship
- Seeking God When Troubled

# Family

"As for me and my family, we will serve the Lord."
• Joshua 24:15 ICB •

_____

Signed

_____

Date

# Family

"But as for me and my household, we will serve the Lord."
• Joshua 24:15 NIV •

Signed

Date

# Salvation in Christ

····························································································

When anyone is in Christ, it is a whole new world.
The old things are gone; suddenly, everything is new!
• 2 Corinthians 5:17 ERV •

_____

Signed

_____

Date

# Salvation in Christ

....................................................................

Therefore, if anyone is in Christ, the new creation has come:
The old has gone, the new is here!
• 2 Corinthians 5:17 NIV •

_____

_____

_____

_____

_____

_____
Signed

_____
Date

# Prayer

"Then you will call my name. You will come to me and pray to me, and I will listen to you. You will search for me, and when you search for me with all your heart, you will find me."
• Jeremiah 29:12-13 ERV •

_____

Signed

_____

Date

# Prayer

........................................................................

"Then you will call on me and come and pray to me, and I will listen to you. You will seek me and find me when you seek me with all your heart."
• Jeremiah 29:12-13 NIV •

_____

_____

_____

_____

_____

_____

Signed

_____

Date

# Rest in the Lord

....................................................

Rest in the LORD, and wait patiently for Him.
• Psalm 37:7 NKJV •

_____

Signed

_____

Date

# Rest in the Lord

My people will live in peaceful dwelling places,
in secure homes, in undisturbed places of rest.
• Isaiah 32:18 NIV •

_____

_____

_____

_____

_____
Signed

_____
Date

# Children and Parents

Children, obey your parents the way the Lord wants,
because this is the right thing to do.
• Ephesians 6:1 ERV •

_____

Signed

_____

Date

# Children and Parents

Children are a gift from the Lord.
• Psalm 127:3 ICB •

_____

Signed

_____

Date

# Faithfulness of God

For great is your love, higher than the heavens;
your faithfulness reaches to the skies.
• Psalm 108:4 NIV •

_____

Signed

_____

Date

# Faithfulness of God

Because of the LORD's great love we are not consumed, for his compassions never fail. They are new every morning; great is your faithfulness.
• Lamentations 3:22-23 NIV •

_____

_____

_____

_____

_____

_____

Signed

_____

Date

# Resting in God
# When Overwhelmed

"Come to me, all of you who are tired and have heavy loads.
I will give you rest."
• Matthew 11:28 ICB •

_____

Signed

_____

Date

"Come to me,
all you who are weary
and burdened, and
I will give you rest."

Matthew 11:28 NIV

# Resting in God When Overwhelmed

. . . . . . . . . . . . . . . . . . . . . . . . . . . . . . . . . . . . . . . . . . . . . . . . . . . . . . . .

"Come to me, all you who are weary and burdened, and I will give you rest."
• Matthew 11:28 NIV •

_____

_____

_____

_____

_____
Signed

_____
Date

# God's Word Is Perfect

Your promises are so sweet to me.
They are like honey to my mouth!
• Psalm 119:103 ICB •

_____
Signed

_____
Date

How SWEET
are your words
to my taste,
SWEETER
than honey
to my mouth!

Psalm 119:103 NIV

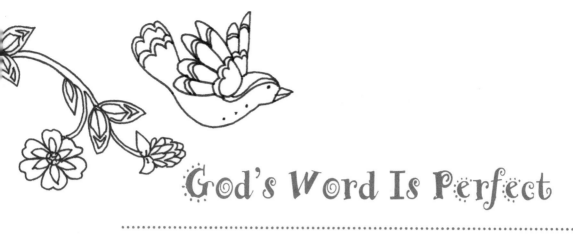

# God's Word Is Perfect

How sweet are your words to my taste,
sweeter than honey to my mouth!
• Psalm 119:103 NIV •

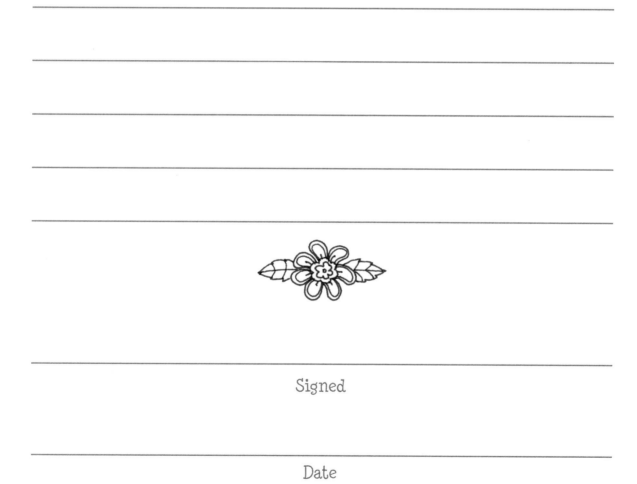

Signed

Date

# Encouragement

So encourage each other and help each other grow
stronger in faith, just as you are already doing.
• 1 Thessalonians 5:11 ERV •

_____

Signed

_____

Date

# Encouragement

Therefore encourage one another and build each other up,
just as in fact you are doing.
• 1 Thessalonians 5:11 NIV •

_____

_____

_____

_____

_____

_____
Signed

_____
Date

# Thankfulness

............................................................

Give thanks no matter what happens.
• 1 Thessalonians 5:18 NIRV •

_____

Signed

_____

Date

# Thankfulness

Rejoice always, pray continually, give thanks in all circumstances;
for this is God's will for you in Christ Jesus.
• 1 Thessalonians 5:16-18 NIV •

_____

_____

_____

_____

_____

_____

Signed

_____

Date

# God's Word Lives Forever

"The grass dies, and the flowers fall.
But the word of our God will live forever."
• Isaiah 40:8 ICB •

_____

Signed

_____

Date

# God's Word Lives Forever

"The grass withers and the flowers fade,
but the word of our God stands forever."
• Isaiah 40:8 NLT •

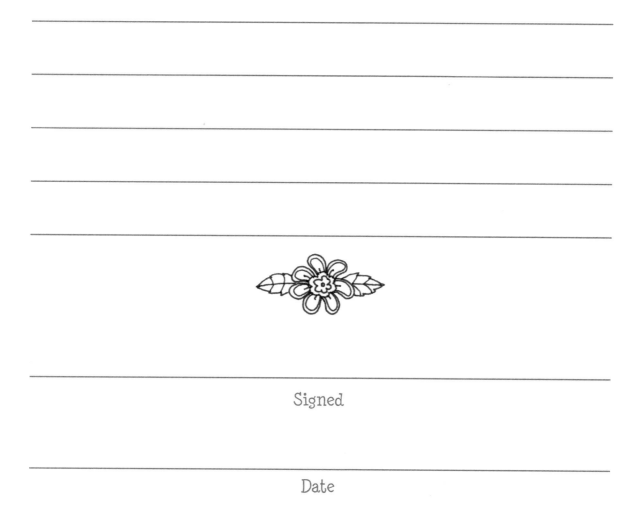

Signed

Date

# Praising God

. . . . . . . . . . . . . . . . . . . . . . . . . . . . . . . . . . . . . . . . . . .

Praise the LORD because he is good. Sing praises to our God.
It is good and pleasant to praise him.
• Psalm 147:1 ERV •

_____

Signed

_____

Date

# Praising God

Praise the LORD. How good it is to sing praises to our God,
how pleasant and fitting to praise him!

• Psalm 147:1 NIV •

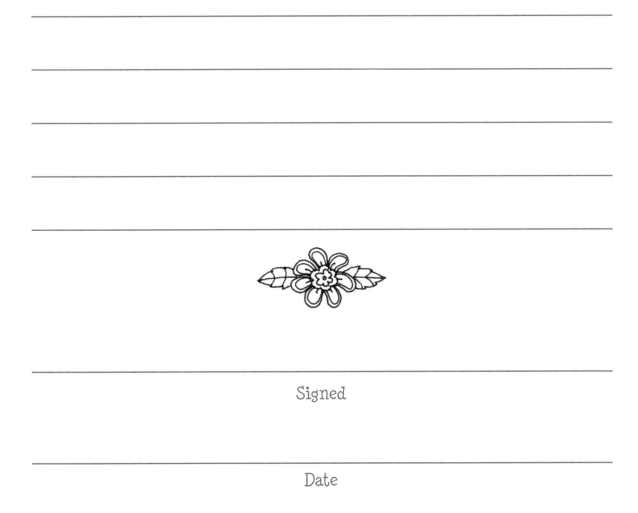

_____

_____

_____

_____

_____

Signed

_____

Date

# Presence of God

You will take my hand and lead me.
• Psalm 139:10 ERV •

Signed

Date

# Presence of God

If I rise on the wings of the dawn, if I settle on the far side of the sea,
even there your hand will guide me, your right hand will hold me fast.
• Psalm 139:9-10 NIV •

_____

_____

_____

_____

_____

Signed

_____

Date

# Trusting in the Lord

· · · · · · · · · · · · · · · · · · · · · · · · · · · · · · · · · · · · · · · · · · · · · · · · · · · ·

But the people who trust the Lord will become strong again.
They will be able to rise up as an eagle in the sky.
They will run without needing rest.
They will walk without becoming tired.
• Isaiah 40:31 ICB •

_____

Signed

_____

Date

# Trusting in the Lord

But those who hope in the LORD will renew their strength.
They will soar on wings like eagles; they will run
and not grow weary, they will walk and not be faint.
• Isaiah 40:31 NIV •

_____

_____

_____

_____

_____

_____
Signed

_____
Date

# Worship

Come, let us bow down and worship him!
Let us kneel before the LORD who made us.
He is our God, and we are the people he cares for,
his sheep that walk by his side.
• Psalm 95:6-7 ERV •

_____

Signed

_____

Date

ASCRIBE TO
THE LORD
THE GLORY DUE
HIS NAME; WORSHIP
THE LORD IN THE
SPLENDOR OF
HIS HOLINESS.

Psalm 29:2 NIV

# Worship

Ascribe to the LORD the glory due his name;
worship the LORD in the splendor of his holiness.
• Psalm 29:2 NIV •

_____

_____

_____

_____

_____

_____

Signed

_____

Date

# God Is Perfect

The Lord's teachings are perfect. They give new strength.
The Lord's rules can be trusted. They make plain people wise.
The Lord's orders are right. They make people happy.
The Lord's commands are pure. They light up the way.
• Psalm 19:7-8 ICB •

_____

Signed

_____

Date

# God Is Perfect

The law of the LORD is perfect, refreshing the soul.
The statutes of the LORD are trustworthy, making wise the simple.
The precepts of the LORD are right, giving joy to the heart.
The commands of the LORD are radiant, giving light to the eyes.
• Psalm 19:7-8 NIV •

_____

_____

_____

_____

_____
Signed

_____
Date

# Loving God

· · · · · · · · · · · · · · · · · · · · · · · · · · · · · · · · · · · · · · · · · ·

"Love the Lord your God with all your heart."
• Matthew 22:37 ERV •

_____

Signed

_____

Date

# Loving God

"Love the Lord your God with all your heart and with all your soul and with all your strength and with all your mind."
• Luke 10:27 NIV •

_____

_____

_____

_____

_____

_____
Signed

_____
Date

# Following God

You will teach me the right way to live. Just being with you will bring complete happiness. Being at your right side will make me happy forever.
• Psalm 16:11 ERV •

_____

Signed

_____

Date

# Following God

You will show me the path of life; in Your presence is fullness of joy;
at Your right hand are pleasures forevermore.

• Psalm 16:11 NKJV •

_____

_____

_____

_____

_____

Signed

_____

Date

# God's Love for Us

The LORD is kind and merciful, patient and full of love.
• Psalm 145:8 ERV •

_____

Signed

_____

Date

# God's Love for Us

The LORD is gracious and compassionate, slow to anger and rich in love.
• Psalm 145:8 NIV •

_____

_____

_____

_____

_____

_____

Signed

_____

Date

# Joy

"So you will go out from there with joy. You will be led out in peace.
When you come to the mountains and hills, they will begin singing.
All the trees in the fields will clap their hands."
• Isaiah 55:12 ERV •

_____

Signed

_____

Date

# Joy

"You will go out in joy and be led forth in peace;
the mountains and hills will burst into song before you,
and all the trees of the field will clap their hands."
• Isaiah 55:12 NIV •

_____

_____

_____

_____

_____

_____

Signed

_____

Date

# Following Jesus

Let us look only to Jesus. He is the one who began our faith,
and he makes our faith perfect.
• Hebrews 12:2 ICB •

_____

Signed

_____

Date

# Following Jesus

We must never stop looking to Jesus. He is the leader of our faith,
and he is the one who makes our faith complete. He suffered death
on a cross. But he accepted the shame of the cross as if it were
nothing because of the joy he could see waiting for him.
And now he is sitting at the right side of God's throne.
• Hebrews 12:2 ERV •

_____

_____

_____

_____

_____

Signed

_____

Date

# Friendship

A friend loves you all the time.
• Proverbs 17:17 ICB •

_____

Signed

_____

Date

# Friendship

A friend loves at all times.
• Proverbs 17:17 NIV •

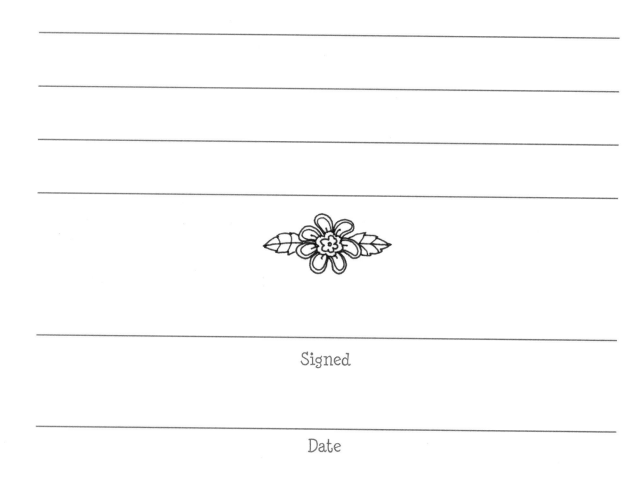

Signed

Date

# Seeking God When Troubled

Like a deer drinking from a stream, I reach out to you, my God.
• Psalm 42:1 ERV •

_____

Signed

_____

Date

# Seeking God When Troubled

As the deer pants for streams of water,
so my soul pants for you, my God.
• Psalm 42:1 NIV •

_____

_____

_____

_____

_____

_____
Signed

_____
Date